From
Grandpa & Grandma

LEFTY'S PLACE

With Special Thanks to

Dr. Alfred Bader; Dr. Theresa Parrott and Staff;
Dr. Geraldine Waxman; Dr. Michael Libenson; Drs. Homer and Judith
Marquit; Deborah and Rebecca; Willy; Maria; Lisa; Dottie;
Dr. Lois Libenson and Class; and all of the other children who,
through their suggestions, helped make this book
more sensitive to their needs.

LEFTY'S PLACE

Written and Illustrated
by Lewis G. Nierman

Kindness
PUBLICATIONS, Inc.
Plantation, Florida

BOOKS TO EDUCATE, ENTERTAIN AND INSPIRE

Library of Congress catalog card number 93-078924

ISBN 0-9636820-0-8

First U.S. Edition
Printed in the U.S.A.
Published in the United States by

Kindness Publications, Inc.
1859 North Pine Island Road
Suite #135
Plantation, Florida 33322

For The Animals

This book is dedicated to Lefty and other animals large and small, domestic and wild, who have enriched our lives and our world.

Thanks to their love, trust, courage and basic goodness, they inspire us to be better humans and to realize our potential for kindness.

INTRODUCTION

Welcome to a world of warm sunshine, plants and many exciting wild birds and animals. It is a beautiful place, but it can also be a dangerous one.

Here you will find a wonderful story of how Rebecca, a young girl who loves all animals, saves Lefty's life. From this she learns much about the importance of all living things and what it means to never give up.

Lefty is actually a wild Muscovy duck who is alive and well today in the State of Florida. Muscovy ducks were brought to live in North America over 100 years ago by people who raised them for food. Now that people don't hunt or eat these ducks, their descendants live wild and free in great numbers on the waters of Florida and the Southeastern United States.

Muscovies may not be the prettiest ducks or the most colorful. The adults are large, mostly black or brown in color with small markings of white or grey. But like Lefty, Muscovies seem to be the smartest and most friendly toward people.

As you enter Rebecca's world and read about Lefty's adventure, remember that he is real. Lefty lives today because of a person's love and kindness and his own courage and hard work.

THE NIGHT VISITS

As she peered through the dark at the clock next to her bed, Rebecca could see it was only three o'clock. Every night for the past two weeks something had awakened her at this same time. Maybe it was a noise - -or maybe just some strange feelings she had. Again, she got herself out of bed and tip-toed down the narrow hall outside her room.

Getting up was usually difficult for Rebecca. Her alarm clock would go off at six o'clock and it would be hard getting ready for school on time each day. For some reason she had no problem getting up for this short trip down to the small bathroom a few feet away. She actually looked forward to it with great excitement.

A small night light was all that lit the bathroom. The cardboard box which rested on the counter near the sink was lined with towels and seemed empty except for the dark shadows inside. Peeking through the door and over the edge, Rebecca looked in to those shadows for some kind of movement.

The movement came just as it always did. A little brown and tan head rose out of the darkness and turned to greet her. The bright round eyes were shining from the small night light bulb. A few tiny "peeps" came from the little fuzzy creature who then tried as hard as possible to stand and face Rebecca.

It was Lefty, a six week old Muscovy duck who had come into her home very much by accident. Now after two weeks of Lefty's life in a box, he and Rebecca would find out about this duck's future later today. It was Lefty's day for another visit to the doctor, the veterinarian who had set his broken right leg in the pink cast which he had worn for fourteen days and nights.

As Rebecca stood next to him for one more nighttime visit, she placed her hand in the box and gently rubbed Lefty under his bill. She had always done this and, as a sign of his love and trust, Lefty nibbled her fingers gently and gave two more little "peeps".

Even though she was only ten years old, Rebecca had become responsible for the care, health and safety of another living creature. She had worked hard to do everything right. Still, she couldn't help but wonder how things were going to turn out and what this last day in a cast would mean for Lefty's future and hers.

LEFTY'S ADVENTURE

Lefty's adventure really began with the arrival of another duck named "Keppy". Keppy was also a Muscovy duck and she joined dozens of other ducks and birds already living on the lake. Keppy was to become Lefty's mother.

Rebecca always thought Keppy was a "girl duck". If she were a "boy" he would be called a "drake". Keppy is a fairly small Muscovy, a little shy and very, very tame. It became more and more certain Keppy was a "girl" in the spring when she would fly in for food each morning then fly off far away out of sight. She would return every morning but not be seen all the rest of the day. She always flew off in the same direction and came back the same way. Something special was certainly happening to change Keppy's life

- -and Rebecca's.

One morning Keppy didn't come for food with all the others. When she didn't come the next day either, Rebecca started worrying that something bad had happened. Was there an accident? Was she hit by a car? Did she get attacked by another animal?

On the third day Rebecca's whole family decided to begin looking. They drove slowly in their car all around the neighborhood to nearby streams, canals and other lakes, but there was no sign of little "Keppy" duck. For two hours they drove in circles. At each turn they got further from their house and lake until they were nearly one mile away across many other streets, lakes, and even a big wide main roadway. Cars and trucks were speeding in both directions and it was on that big roadway that Rebecca and her family found their missing friend. They finally knew absolutely, positively that Keppy was a girl duck.

KEPPY'S SURPRISE

Rebecca's father stopped their car in the middle of the roadway as Keppy and fifteen one-day-old baby ducklings made their way across one side of the highway. Once they reached the safety of grass that divided the road, they rested for a few seconds, and toddled into the road again. The babies followed Keppy all the way to the other side of the street.

Lots of people stopped to watch. They waited patiently as mother duck and fifteen waddling ducklings finally made it to safety.

The question now was, where were Keppy and her new babies going? The babies were obediently following their mother on some new journey. Rebecca watched them hop, scoot and scurry. She soon began to realize that Keppy's plan was to move her new family to Rebecca's yard - -the place where she knew they would be safest.

For the next four weeks, all went well for the family of new ducks. Life on the lake for Keppy, Lefty and his brothers and sisters had been safe and happy. Lefty was a cute little guy looking like all the other little ones. They were all small brown and tan bundles of fuzz and just as cute as could be. It was impossible to tell one duck from the other at that age, until Lefty had his accident.

THE ACCIDENT

It happened one afternoon when Rebecca arrived home from school. Birds and ducks were waiting all around the house for their regular food treats, and others came swimming, flying and running from all around the lake.

Keppy arrived with all the others, her tiny babies close behind. Somehow when it came to food, even the littlest ducks and birds managed to brave the dangers of the large feet, wings and bills of older ducks. The smallest duckling was always tough enough and fast enough to get its share too.

Every afternoon Rebecca sat on the grass with all the ducks and fed them bread. They came close and even climbed on her to get the treats.

On this special day Rebecca noticed something different about one baby while watching Keppy and her family come to greet her from across the lake. They all swam in their usual close little group, but one kept falling behind. When they reached the shore, they all climbed out; all except one who couldn't get up the steep edge. He stayed by himself in the water as the rest came for treats. Lefty couldn't make it.

Maybe it was because he fell or got bumped by a larger duck? Maybe he got tangled in a rock or the roots of a tree? Whatever the reason, Lefty was in great danger.

Rebecca watched him in the water as he swam with only his left leg. The right one didn't move and was stretched out behind him. From what Rebecca had learned about ducks and wild animals, an injured baby who couldn't keep up with the group would probably not survive. He would soon get separated from the others and then probably be attacked, injured or killed by bigger animals called predators.

Predators can be birds, like hawks, or even ground animals like a raccoon or fox. This happens in the wild because it is the way nature works. Rebecca could understand and respect that, but when it happened in her backyard it was different.

These are animals Rebecca had grown to love. Lefty was not just a wild baby duck. After all, she had watched the babies grow. She had fed them and cared for them and because of that, she felt more responsible for their safety.

TO THE RESCUE

Catch Me If You Can

The first thing Rebecca had to do was catch Lefty. This was not an easy job even though he moved with only one leg. His fear made him very strong and fast. All his instincts told him he had to get away and survive.

She moved toward him and tried to catch him with a large net from her swimming pool. He was so frightened he dashed off into the water. Using his one good leg, he climbed up on land a few feet away.

Limping along as fast as he could, he scampered under a lime tree, but Rebecca was still able to catch him easily. Lefty's right leg was broken. That's why he's been called "Lefty" ever since.

Taking him out of the net, Rebecca held him for a while until he didn't seem so frightened. She put him in a box lined with soft towels and fed him some fresh grasses while she waited for her mom and dad to come home. There wasn't much else she could do but pet him. It made Lefty feel better and made her feel better too. The rest would be up to the doctor.

VETERINARIAN

LEFTY'S DOCTOR

Lefty's doctor, also known as a veterinarian, was a wonderful woman who made them feel good about helping Lefty. She examined Lefty and took x-rays to see about the broken leg. She talked to him softly and held him very gently. For a while he made peeping sounds but he was more afraid than in pain.

She fixed his broken bone and put it in a small pink cast very much like the way the doctor fixed Rebecca's broken arm last year - - except her cast was white so her friends could write silly stuff on it.

Rebecca felt happy the doctor's visit was over but she felt sad for Lefty. He would be in the cast for a few weeks and have to stay still in his little box. She wondered how frightened he was. How could he possibly understand what was happening to him? Did he know this was best for him? Was he mad at her for catching him? How could he possibly know she still loved him?

A TIME TO HEAL

The biggest question was, "would Lefty be all right?" Would he be as good as new when the leg healed? Would it heal? No one knew. Not even the veterinarian could be sure because the break was very bad. Lefty was very young, and duck leg bones often don't heal just as good as new. There was a chance that Lefty might heal perfectly or that he might not heal at all. They would have to wait.

For the next two weeks Lefty was to have a new place. He had gone through a painful and tiring experience being handled, poked, examined and put in a cast! His comfortable place in the wild had now been changed to a tiny box in a room filled with strange sights and sounds.

During that time, Lefty got all of Rebecca's extra time and attention. She got up a little earlier each morning and stayed up a little later each night just to be with him.

Even during school, her thoughts were always about Lefty in his little box. At times it was even hard to listen to the teacher's words and right after school she came straight home. She missed playing with her friends, but to her it was worth it.

LEFTY'S BIG DAY

Finally, the two weeks of resting and healing were over. The day of Lefty's return visit to the doctor was here. Rebecca's heart raced with a mixture of excitement and fear.

She spent the ride home from school that day thinking about Lefty as always. When it was her stop, Rebecca was off the bus, in the house, down the hall and into Lefty's room in a flash. He was up and moving around as if he knew big things were going to happen soon. She held him gently, rubbed his neck the way he loved and changed his towels and food one more time. After quickly feeding the other animals outside, she changed her clothes and waited patiently for her mom and dad to get home.

Everyone in Rebecca's family had helped take care of Lefty at one time or another. On this day, even Rebecca's big brother went along for the ride to the veterinarian. They all waited patiently during the examination and listened with great excitement to the doctor's words.

After two weeks in the cast, Lefty's leg did get a little better, but the doctor said it would never be perfect. Lefty would always have a bent leg and foot and always walk with a limp. He would never be strong enough or fast enough to protect himself from predators. He was always going to need Rebecca's care if he was to live a full life.

Could she do it? Could Rebecca give Lefty a chance at life and happiness? Lefty would always have to be with his "human family". He would not be able to do all the things he would have done if he hadn't been hurt, but at least he would be alive, happy and as close to the wild as possible. The decision was an easy one for her to make.

LEFTY: THE "I CAN DO IT" DUCK

Rebecca made up her mind to finish the job she had started - -the job of helping Lefty be the best, strongest, happiest duck his broken leg would let him be.

The job wasn't going to be easy. Over the next few months Lefty grew quickly from little baby duckling to big Muscovy duck. He needed many things including good food, bigger and bigger boxes for sleeping, and finally a big special house of his own.

Lefty's
PLACE

By the time Lefty was four months old, he had already grown to almost full size. He was much bigger than all his brothers and sisters and no box was large enough for sleeping. The little swims he took in the bath tub for exercise when he was small were now done outside in the big pool. All that time Lefty had been a busy duck going through a lot of hard work designed to help him get strong again . . . and Lefty really did it!

Lefty does most of the things a duck is supposed to do on his own now. He can walk, but slowly and with a limp. In the swimming pool, where he exercises and plays every day, he swims and dives as well as any duck. His house, which is called "Lefty's Place", is kept by the pool. Lefty sleeps and eats protected from danger by wire screens.

Every day Rebecca still changes his towels, gives him fresh food, and lots of time to swim and play. She carries him over to the grass each morning and evening so he can greet his buddies and feed with them outside. He's not lonesome because all the ducks know him and spend all day just a few feet outside the screened fence. She still wakes up many nights at three o'clock to check on him too.

Rebecca is very proud of Lefty. She knows how hard he tries. Who would have ever thought he could walk, run, swim, dive, get in and out of the pool, and even put himself to bed at sunset? He always seems to be saying "I CAN DO IT!"

A HAPPY LIFE

Lefty will never be what some people call "perfect". He won't be able to live on his own like other ducks. But he always tries. He does things his own way and isn't that what is most important?

Lots of animals, just like lots of people, have things happen to them. Sometimes they are just born differently. Sometimes they become sick or injured. Like Lefty, they have to learn, and practice, and try to be the best they can. They need a chance to enjoy their lives and be happy. Thanks to the encouragement and care from Rebecca and her family, Lefty was able to do it.

Now, each day as she is with her animal friends in the backyard, Rebecca sees much more than before. Instead of just seeing cute and cuddly creatures doing different and entertaining things, she sees life. The animals which had always seemed interesting but different from people, now seem to be much more like Rebecca than she thought.

Lefty's accident, his pain, his fear and his need for help are no different from an injured person's needs. His need for love and kindness is just the same. His hard work to stay alive, be strong and get better is just the same as a person's should be.

Rebecca also sees that while we are alike in many ways, we each have wonderful differences. She now knows that Lefty is not only a duck, but he is also special in his own way. She sees that the world is filled with animals of all kinds, shapes and colors. Each one has its place and they all should be protected and enjoyed.

Lefty was always lucky enough to be surrounded by kind, gentle, caring people. Fortunately for Lefty, now his place will always be with Rebecca.